GO
COM

By

J. DANSON SMITH

Author of "100 Best Loved Poems"
"Songs In The Night" etc.

Published by

B. McCall Barbour

28 George IV Bridge, Edinburgh EH1 1ES, Scotland

Printed January 1986

ISBN 0 7132 0030 8

Cover picture by Whiteholme of Dundee

Printed by Stanley L. Hunt (Printers) Ltd., Midland Road, Rushden, Northants

GOD . . . WHO COMFORTETH.

" The God of all comfort ; Who comforteth us in all our tribulation, that we may be able to comfort them which are in any trouble, by the comfort wherewith we ourselves are comforted of God."—II Cor. i. 3, 4.

" God, that COMFORTETH those that are cast down, comforted us."—II Cor. vii. 6.

" As one whom his mother comforteth, so will I comfort you."—Is. lxvi. 13.

" He hath sent Me . . . to comfort all that mourn."—Is. lxi. 1, 2.

TO whom shall we go with our sorrow and anguish ?
To whom shall we go with our hunger and pain ?
To whom shall we go when, grief-stricken, we languish ?
To whom shall we go and not find it but vain ?

Can He read the sorrow, can He feel the heart-ache ?
Can He understand and interpret my grief ?
Can He share my anguish, my loss and my heart-break ?
Can He enter in—and can He give relief ?

" The God of all comfort " ! Then, surely He'll aid me,
If broken and bleeding I but to Him come :
He knows me, and loves me,—yea, He Himself made me,
And in His great heart He has got for me room.

He shareth my sorrow,—my need He full knoweth ;
My wound He can heal with His wonderful balm ;
And into my torrent of grief from Him floweth,
The exquisite sense of an infinite calm.

THOU GOEST WITH US.

" Thou goest with us."—Ex. xxxiii. 16.

" My presence shall go with thee, and I will give thee rest."—Ex. xxxiii. 14.

" Lo, I am with you alway."—Matt. xxviii. 20.

" He hath said, I will never leave thee, nor forsake thee." —Heb. xiii. 5.

THOU goest with us ! This would be our comfort !
Thou goest with us, on life's further way !
Thou goest with us, on into the future !
Thou goest with us,—with us, day by day !

Thou goest *with* us ! not alone we journey,—
Not at *our* charges take we to the road !
Thou goest with us,—guiding, guarding, caring !
Thou goest with us,—cov'nant-keeping God !

Thou goest with us, through each lonesome valley !
Thou goest with us,—through our blackest night !
Thou goest with us,—through each crushing sorrow !
Also to help us scale each rugged height !

Thou goest with us ! This our peace and portion !
We are with Thee,—our spirits thus have rest !
What though full much, unwelcome, may attend us,
Since thus with Thee we are supremely blest.

HE KNOWETH THE WAY.

" He knoweth the way that I take."—Job xxiii. 10.
" The LORD knoweth the way of the righteous."—Ps. i. 6.
" He knoweth what is in the darkness."—Dan. ii. 22.
" He that is perfect in knowledge is with thee."—Job xxxvi. 4.
" Your Father knoweth."—Matt. vi. 8.

THE way that I take—it is still veiled in darkness ;
Whereunto it leadeth I cannot yet tell ;
But since *He* doth know,—and doth lead,—it means blessing,—
And heart may believingly say " All is well."

The way that I take, though it rough be and rugged,
Perchance is more blest than a road smooth and plain :
He knoweth the way, in His great plan of blessing,
That best can work out truest spiritual gain.

The way that I take—though enshrouded in darkness,—
In darkness to me, unto God is not dim ;
The darkness to me may itself be a blessing,
If only it makes me walk closer with Him.

The way that I take ! This my comfort—" He knoweth " !
And He—my great Father,—doth tenderly care ;
And over life's way, and its miles, and its journey,
My feet He can guide, and my life He can bear.

No need then for having long stretches of vision ;
One step at a time may be sweeter—more blest ;
Dependence on Him by this process will deepen,
So, too, by this process will deepen His rest.

MY ABIDING PORTION.

" Thou art my portion, O LORD."—Ps. cxix. 57.

" The LORD is my portion, saith my soul ; therefore will I hope in Him."—La. iii. 24.

" Whom have I in heaven but Thee ? and there is none upon earth that I desire beside Thee. My flesh and my heart faileth : but God is the strength of my heart, and my PORTION for ever."—Ps. lxxiii. 25, 26.

GONE are the years,—the brightest and most golden,
Rich in their comforts, laden with their bliss ;
Full to repleteness with their favoured blessings,—
Blessings which now my heart doth truly miss.

Gone is the strength which once so freely carried
My nimble feet, where will would have them go
With voice to sing, or heart and hands to succour,—
Work, with its joys, I may no longer know.

Gone, too, are those,—to me so deeply precious,—
Parts of my life I now so strangely miss ;
Leaving a sense of vacant incompleteness,—
Not to be filled with aught of earthly bliss.

But, though the years have gone, with all their blessing,
Though strength and substance both have sadly failed,—
Though those whom God once gave He now hath taken,
And all the lights, which cheered me once, have paled,—

Still, I have God,—and, having Him,—my portion,—
Sharing His love, and trusting in His Word,—
Life still is sweet, and rich with wondrous blessing,—
And I enjoy the goodness of the Lord.

IT IS GOOD FOR ME.

" It is good for me that I have been afflicted ; that I might learn Thy statutes."—Ps. cxix. 71.

" As for you, ye thought evil against me ; but God meant it unto GOOD."—Ge. l. 20.

" The LORD thy God . . . Who led thee through that great and terrible wilderness . . . Who fed thee . . . with manna, . . . that He might humble thee, and that He might prove thee, to do thee GOOD at thy latter end."—De. viii. 14-16.

" The LORD blessed the latter end of Job more than his beginning."—Job xlii. 12.

'TIS good for me ! What ? That I've been afflicted ?
Can good e'er come from shadowed things of pain ?
From days and ways—so burdened and restricted ?
How can such things be countenanced as gain ?

'Tis good for me—if these have drawn HIM nearer,—
If He has been my solace and my calm :
'Tis good for me—if by these things He's dearer ;
If His near presence is my spirit's balm.

'Tis good for me—if things which seemed disaster
Have stayed my steps—which else had gone astray ;
'Tis good for me, if, owning Him as Master,—
I now can gladly let Him have His way.

'Tis good for me ! And when, at last, in Glory,
When much of mystery still—is clear and plain,—
When we may read life's full and final story,
Affliction will be seen as meant for gain.

BLEEDING TO BLESS.

" Always bearing about in the body the dying of the Lord Jesus, that the life also of Jesus might be made manifest in our body. For we which live are alway delivered unto death for Jesus' sake, that the life also of Jesus might be made manifest in our mortal flesh. So then death worketh in us, but life in you."—II Co. iv. 10-12.

" If, when ye do well, and suffer for it, ye take it patiently, this is acceptable with God. For even hereunto were ye called : because Christ also suffered for us, leaving us an example, that ye should follow His steps. . . . Who, when He was reviled, reviled not again ; when He suffered, He threatened not ; but committed Himself (His cause, *Marg.*) to Him that judgeth righteously."—I Pe. ii. 20-23.

" Unto you it is given in the behalf of Christ, not only to believe on Him, but also to suffer for His sake."—Phi. i. 29.

" Be thou partaker of the afflictions of the Gospel."—II. Ti. i. 8.

DEEP sorrows come,—and grief and tears :
Sore sufferings—as pass the years ;
And many forms of keen distress,
Perhaps that we may others bless.

Joys wished for—which we well might choose,
Yet somehow have to yield and lose,—
Things costing much—did we confess—
Perhaps that we might others bless.

And things unwanted come our way ;
Unwelcome, yet they somehow stay ;
And earth-joys fade—grow less and less,—
Perhaps that we may others bless.

It seems the way ; the track of years
Where life-blood spilt so oft appears,—
'Tis there we learn how to express
The things and thoughts which others bless.

BE OF GOOD COURAGE.

" Be strong and of a good courage ; be not afraid, neither be thou dismayed : for the LORD thy God is with thee whithersoever thou goest."—Jos. i. 9.

" In nothing terrified by your adversaries : which (*your fearlessness*) is to them an evident token of perdition, but to you of salvation, and that of God."—Phi. i. 28.

" Greater is He that is in you, than he that is in the world." —I John iv. 4.

" Thanks be unto God, which always causeth us to triumph in Christ."—II Co. ii. 14.

BE of good courage as the conflict thickens,—
The ceaseless warfare, growing yet more strong ;
The endless fight, which wears, unnerves and sickens ;
The combat which, unslacking, lasteth long.

Be of good courage 'neath the crushing pressure,
Which more and more saints feel o'er all the earth :
Opposing forces ; weight beyond all measure ;
New forms of evil,—ever springing forth.

Be of good courage, as the darkness deepens,—
The darkness which, most sure, o'er earth doth spread :
The moral darkness ! that which virtue cheapens !
Dark shadow of the deeper dark ahead.

And whence the courage that will never fail thee ?
Not human—though most noble, true and strong !
Thy place in Christ triumphant will avail thee,—
And conqueror make thee o'er the foes who throng.

THEY SANG AN HYMN.

" And when they had sung an hymn, they went out into the Mount of Olives."—Matt. xxvi. 30.

" Not forsaking the assembling of ourselves together."—He. x. 25.

" At midnight Paul and Silas prayed, and sang praises unto God. . . . And suddenly there was a great earthquake, . . . all the doors were opened, and every one's bands were loosed." —Ac. xvi. 25, 26.

THAT darkest night an hymn they sang;
Dear fitting close to that first feast!
Their strong, male voices nobly rang,—
Nor would the Saviour's voice be least.

They sang an hymn! Did He design
Their drooping spirits thus to raise?
They sang some simple psalm divine!
Were richer through united praise.

We, too, might sing, though much distressed,
Nor dumbly wait till cometh light;
We surely would be richly blest,
Through bravely singing in our " night."

" They sang an hymn!" We, too, may choose
To raise the voice though heart be sad;
Blest means if thus our load we lose,
And find our spirits strangely glad.

HELP, LORD !

" Help, LORD ; for the godly man ceaseth; for the faithful fail from among the children of men."—Ps. xii. 1.

" This poor man cried, and the LORD heard him, and saved him out of all his troubles."—Ps. xxxiv. 6.

" The eyes of the LORD are upon the righteous, and His ears are open unto their cry."—Ps. xxxiv. 15.

" Call upon Me in the day of trouble : I will deliver thee, and thou shalt glorify Me."—Ps. l. 15.

HELP, Lord ! Our hearts would, stricken, seek Thine aid ;
Thou hast all power, we therefore to Thee cry :
" Help, Lord "—brief utt'rance, boldly, swiftly made ;
" Help, Lord " we urge,—and safe on Thee rely.

" Help, Lord ! " He hears,—whate'er may be our need,
If wilful sin doth not block up the way ;
And if He hears 'tis sure that He will heed,—
And to His child will come without delay.

" Help, Lord ! " That's all ! The rest He knows full well,—
All that doth press, depress, oppress, He knows ;
Pressure, perchance, words cannot fully tell,—
Onslaught of evil from the spirit's foes !

" Help, Lord ! " He hears ! He heeds ! He sends again !
If need be, angels sends,—to make us strong :
Would wed His Word, yea, with our faith, and then
Teach us to sing a triumph spirit song.

IF GOD BE FOR US.

" If God be for us, who can be against us ? "—Ro. viii. 31.

" He that toucheth you toucheth the apple of His eye."—Zec. ii. 8.

" The LORD is on my side ; I will not fear : what can man do unto me ? The LORD taketh my part with them that help me."—Ps. cxviii. 6, 7.

" The LORD taketh pleasure in His people."—Ps. cxlix. 4.

" IF God be for us ! "—why, my soul, be fearful ?
" If God be for us "—who against can be ?
If we are His,—and living in His purpose,
All counter-wills are mere futility.

" If God be for us ! " God ! supremely sovereign !
'Gainst Whom no will can e'er have final sway,—
If *God* be for us—then both rest and refuge
Our hearts may have,—for He shall have His way.

" If God be *for us* "—He Who loves His children,—
He Who works for them—always for the best,—
Since He is *for us*—songs should be our portion,—
For, in all states, we surely shall be blest.

" If God be for us ! " Shout ! Ring out the challenge !
If God be for us—none against can be !
No one and naught,—however evil seeming,
Can thwart His will, or change His blest decree.

NOT KNOWING WHITHER.

" By faith Abraham, when he was called to go out into a place which he should after receive for an inheritance, obeyed ; and he went out, not knowing whither he went."—He. xi. 8.

" Thou wilt shew me the path of life."—Ps. xvi. 11.

" I being in the way, the Lord led me."—Ge. xxiv. 27.

" NOT knowing whither "—yet, he went,—
One slender promise for his rest :
" A land that I will shew thee " meant
Where e'er it was it would be best.

" Not knowing whither " ! Thus faith grew ;
A clinging hand was raised to God :
And life became at once all new,
And strangely bright became the road.

Not knowing whither ! Thus God's will
Began accomplishèd to be :
Fulfilment grew, and grew, until
A race came—great with destiny.

Not knowing whither ! Soul, fear not !
When He leads out it is to bless !
Abandon fear and anxious thought,
The way leads on to blessedness.

Not knowing whither ! *He* doth know,—
Thy God, thy Guide, thy Guard, thy Friend :
He step by step the way will shew,
Right on unto the journey's end.

Not knowing whither ! This thy rest ;
Thy joy ; thy calm ; thine ease from care :
Led thus thou shalt be truly blest,—
And shalt God's highest purpose share.

EMPTY— ?

" From the end of the earth will I cry unto Thee, when my heart is OVERWHELMED : lead me to the Rock that is higher than I."—Ps. lxi. 2.

" When my father and my mother forsake me, then the LORD will take me (gather me, *Marg.*) up."—Ps. xxvii. 10.

" The LORD . . . hath sent Me to bind up the broken-hearted . . . to comfort all that mourn ; to appoint unto them that mourn in Zion, to give unto them beauty for ashes, the oil of joy for mourning, the garment of praise for the spirit of heaviness."—Is. lxi. 1-3.

" His disciples came, and took up the body, and buried it, and went and TOLD JESUS."—Mat. xiv. 12.

EMPTY homes, and empty places ;
Missing now—the dear loved faces ;
Gone the presences *so* cherished ;
Happy bonds—but now all perished !

Empty hearts—now sadly aching ;
Empty lives—with sore grief breaking :
Empty purposes ! zest gone—
Where the life is sad and lone.

Empty— ? Yes,—but He can fill them ;
With new joys can even thrill them ;
Fill the void and vacant spaces,
Light the dark and lonely places.

Empty— ? Yet He has renewing,—
Lifting—for our sad undoing ;
For the broken—balm and blessing ;
For the weary—sweet refreshing.

Shall we bring our hearts *so* empty
That He fill them with His plenty ?
Shall we let Him change our sadness
Into wondrous selfless gladness ?
Shall we come ? He waits to bless !
To fill up all emptiness.

EVERLASTING ARMS.

" The Eternal God is thy refuge (dwelling-place, R.V.), and underneath are the everlasting arms."—De. xxxiii. 27.

" He shall feed His flock like a shepherd : He shall gather the lambs with His arm, and carry them in His bosom, and shall gently lead those that are with young."—Is. xl. 11.

" In all their affliction He was afflicted, and the angel of His presence saved them : in His love and in His pity He redeemed them ; and He bare them, and carried them all the days of old."—Is. lxiii. 9.

UNDERNEATH and Everlasting,
There are arms outstretched to-day ;
Arms—all other arms contrasting,
In that they can ne'er give way.

Arms, which reach down 'neath life's sorrow,
Fold us in their fond embrace ;
Arms which, on our darkest morrow,
Yet may be our nestling-place.

Arms which cannot,—dare not fail us,—
Arms which ne'er can weary grow,
Arms which, when dark hosts assail us,
Still are 'neath us,—still below.

Such the arms which now enfold thee,
Press thee close to Jesus' breast ;—
Which, in all life's days, would hold thee,
And, in holding, give thee rest.

NO LOOKING BACK.

" This one thing I do, forgetting those things which are behind, and reaching forth unto those things which are before, I press toward the mark for the prize of the high calling of God in Christ Jesus."—Phi. iii. 13, 14.

" By faith Moses, when he was come to years, refused to be called the Son of Pharaoh's daughter ; choosing rather to suffer affliction with the people of God, than to enjoy the pleasures of sin for a season ; esteeming the reproach of Christ greater riches than the treasures in Egypt : for he had respect unto the recompence of the reward."—He. xi. 24-26.

NO looking back ! It might but mean disaster !
No sad regrets o'er costly choices made !
The costlier path was chosen for the Master,—
It was for HIM the sacrifice was paid.

No looking back on what may seem lost treasure,—
At gilded joys, which, seen, were yet not known :
Joys more abiding, and in fuller measure,
Will yet be thine, when earth-born joys have flown.

No looking back, save on the way He led thee ;
Beholding, now, His goodness more and more ;
Reviewing all the means by which He fed thee,
The hearts, the loves, the lives that were His store.

No looking back ! Just forward to the Glory ;
With joyous hope, with glad, expectant face ;
To find, when He unfolds life's finished story,
Wealth,—wealth unfading,—and an honoured place.

NOT IN VAIN.

" Therefore, my beloved brethren, be ye stedfast, unmovable, always abounding in the work of the Lord, forasmuch as ye know that your labour is not in vain in the Lord."—I Co. xv. 58.

" God is not unrighteous to forget your work and labour of love, which ye have shewed toward His name, in that ye have ministered to the saints, and do minister."—He. vi. 10.

" They which run in a race run all. . . . They . . . to obtain a corruptible crown ; but we an incorruptible. I therefore so run, not as uncertainly."—I Co. ix. 24-26.

" I have fought a good fight, I have finished my course, I have kept the faith : henceforth there is laid up for me . . . " —II Ti. iv. 7, 8.

" NOT in vain "—thy work, O noble toiler,
Though scant the fruitage thou dost meanwhile see ;
If wrought, controlled, and guided by the Spirit,
How truly great will yet the harvest be.

" Not in vain "—O silent, suffering servant !
Thy Lord beholds,—and all to Him is known !
Not vain,—nor valueless, the sore affliction,
If by its means Christ more in thee is shewn.

" Not in vain "—O sorely tried believer,—
Though crushing blows upon thee may descend :
He trusts with trials those who can Him honour,—
Whose faith in Him no blows can e'er offend.

" Not in vain "—devout and faithful follower,—
The quiet witness which thy life doth bear :
Nor yet in vain the message of the radiance
Which those abiding in Him ever wear.

IF THOU HADST BEEN HERE.

" Lord, if Thou hadst been here, my brother had not died." —Jno. xi. 21.

" Will the Lord cast off for ever ? and will He be favourable no more ? Is His mercy clean gone for ever ? Doth His promise fail for evermore ? Hath God FORGOTTEN TO BE GRACIOUS ? Hath He in anger shut up His tender mercies ? . . . And I said, This is my infirmity."—Ps. lxxvii. 7-10.

" The just shall live by faith."—Ga. iii. 11.

" IF Thou hadst been here," she complainingly uttered,—
" If Thou hadst been here, then he should not have died ! "
Her faith in His *power* ne'er wavered an instant,—
But His love and His wisdom she almost denied.

We, too, oft go blundering into some challenge !
" If Thou hadst been here," we so erringly say,—
Forgetful that He hath unceasing love for us,
Though sometimes His " comings " are marked by delay.

How blest that our challenges change not His kindness !
Our words,—oft against Him, He gently unheeds !
He keeps on His course of beneficent working,—
Yea, working for *us*, though His heart o'er us bleeds.

" If Thou hadst been here ! "—But He *is* here, and always !
If we are redeemed—then He *is* here to bless,—
To guide, to direct,—to console, and to comfort,—
To join in our joys, and to share our distress.

IF THE LORD WOULD— !

" If the Lord would make windows in heaven, might this thing be ? "—II Ki. vii. 2.

" He performeth the thing that is appointed for me."— Job xxiii. 14.

" For this thing I besought the Lord thrice, that it might depart from me. And He said unto me, My grace is sufficient for thee."—II Co. xii. 8, 9.

" Your Father knoweth what things ye have need of."— Matt. vi. 8.

IF the Lord would—— ! Would what ?
Make windows in heaven for me,—
My burdens would then remove,
And then—I could joyful be.

If the Lord would—— ! Would what ?
Would send all I *think* I need,—
Why, then I should have no want—
Should satisfied be indeed.

If the Lord would—— ! Would what ?
Take all of my pains away,
Why, then I should serve Him well,
And joy in my ministry !

" If the Lord would ! " we sigh ;
Yet better to trust and rest :
Since we are His sheep, why then,
We must be at all times blest.

ARE YE NOT BETTER?

" Behold the fowls of the air : for they sow not, neither do they reap, nor gather into barns ; yet your heavenly Father feedeth them. Are ye not much better than they ? "—Matt. vi. 26.

" Casting all your care upon Him ; for He careth for you."—I Pe. v. 7.

" Behold, I have graven thee upon the palms of my hands." —Is. xlix. 16.

" Can a woman forget her sucking child, that she should not have compassion on the son of her womb ? Yea, they may forget, yet will I not forget thee."—Is. xlix. 15.

HE feedeth them—the Heavenly Father feedeth—
The birds which cannot reap nor store away :
And to our care-worn spirits comes the challenge—
" Are ye not better,—better far than they ? "

Are ye not better than the meaner creatures—
The barnless birds—whom He feeds day by day ?
The house-top sparrow, or the woodland pigeon
" Are ye not better,—better far than they ? "

Are ye not better ? Soul of mine, give answer !
If He feeds *them*,—for thee can His care stay ?
If He for these,—His little creatures,—careth,
Are ye not better,—better far than they ?

Are ye not better ? Rise ! Respond ! Take courage !
Thy faithless fear.—thy dread,—cast far away :
He feedeth them—His fragile, feathered creatures,—
And ye are better,—better far than they !

LOVE NEVER FAILETH.

" Charity (love) suffereth long, and is kind ; . . . Beareth all things, believeth all things, hopeth all things, endureth all things.—Charity NEVER FAILETH."—I Co. xiii. 4-8.

" Having loved His own which were in the world, He loved them unto the end " (" to the uttermost," *R.V., Marg.*) **— Jno. xiii. 1.**

" I have loved thee with an EVERLASTING LOVE."— Je. xxxi. 3.

" We know that we have passed from death unto life, because we love the brethren."—I Jno. iii. 14.

" Beloved, let us love one another : for love is of God."— I Jno. iv. 7.

LOVE never faileth ! Patience may outwear,
And hope and faith themselves at last may pale ;
But love endures, and with all things doth bear,
And darkest things can never make it fail.

Love never faileth ! Never ! Never ! No !
But where shall love that faileth not be found ?
Not 'mongst the flowers which human hearts can grow,
It springeth not from merely nature's ground.

Is HE not love ! He doth not cast me off
When I so sadly fail or go astray :
He doth not mock, deride, nor taunt, nor scoff ;
He woos me back,—then cleanses all away.

And He this love unfailing can impart,
Since I am His, through dear redeeming grace ;
Can flood His love through all my new-born heart,
And speak it out through tone, and touch, and face.

WISHED FOR THE DAY.

" Fearing lest they should have fallen upon rocks, they cast four anchors out of the stern, and WISHED FOR THE DAY."—Ac. xxvii. 29.

" Would God it were morning ! "—De. xxviii. 67.

" Weeping may endure for a night, but joy cometh in the morning."—Ps. xxx. 5.

" The morning cometh."—Is. xxi. 12.

" Even a morning without clouds."—II Sa. xxiii. 4.

TWAS darkest night ! The winds and waves were shrieking ;
Their barque might to the cruel rocks fall prey :
They anchors cast, with spirits torn and fearful,
And anxiously they " wished—wished for the day."

And morning came,—for dawn the dark doth follow,—
The day-break which succeeds the blackest night !
No words can pen the solace and the succour
Which come, to anxious watchers, with the light.

Perhaps we, too, on angry seas are tossing,
And darkest night doth make us wish for day ;
Perhaps we, too, are filled with dark forebodings,—
An anxious fearfulness, a blank dismay.

Will day-break come ? Ah ! sure, and sweet, and blessèd !
Nor need we " wish " for it, for come it must :
And darkest nights and roughest seas afford us
But means to place in Him our noblest trust.

WEARIED WITH HIS JOURNEY.

" Jesus, . . . being wearied with His journey, sat thus on the well."—Jno. iv. 6.

" He said unto them, Come ye yourselves apart into a desert place, and rest a while : for there were many coming and going, and they had no leisure so much as to eat."—Mar. vi. 31.

" When the even was come, He saith unto them, Let us pass over unto the other side. . . . And He was in the hinder part of the ship, asleep on a pillow. . . . And they came over unto the other side of the sea. . . . And when He was come out of the ship, immediately there met Him out of the tombs a man with an unclean spirit."—Mar. iv. 35-41, v. 1, 2.

" WEARIED with His journey," He, the Lord, sat down
At a well of water, out beyond the town ;—
Tired in limb, and foot-sore,—there He found a rest ;
There He, while thus resting, also found a guest.

Where shall end the story,—who on earth can tell,—
Of that hour of converse, yonder at the well ?
Sin disclosed, grew hateful,—peace and power were given,—
And the soul so sin-stained, fit became for Heaven.

" Wearied with His journey " ! We, His children, too,
Wearied with *our* journey, must find strength anew,—
Resting by the wayside,—sitting by some well,—
Staying from our journey, for a brief, brief spell.

Maybe, as we tarry, someone will draw nigh,
Scarred, beyond the hiding, with sin's misery ;
Then, oh, then, to serve Him,—then to meet our guest,—
Words of help to tender ;—pardon, peace, and rest.

BE COMFORTED.

" For I would that ye knew what great conflict I have for . . . them . . . that their hearts might be comforted. . . . " —Col. ii. 1, 2.

" Blessed be God . . . the Father of mercies, and the God of all comfort ; Who comforteth us in all our tribulation."—II Co. i. 3, 4.

" I will not leave you comfortless : I will come to you."—Jno. xiv. 18.

" I, even I, am He that comforteth you."—Is. li. 12.

BE comforted ! " How can I? " hast thou asked?
" When all so precious has been snatched away,—
When love, so tender, hath for ever passed,
And life ebbs out so slow, so wearily."

Be comforted,—though skies be dark o'erhead !
Though life be shorn of much most truly-blest !
Tears are the meat of souls uncomforted ;
Peace is the portion—where they know His rest.

Be comforted ! In God thy comfort lies !
If He doth pain—He also would console ;
The anodyne which soothes—just He supplies ;
He, He alone, the wounded can make whole.

The word is His ! Nor will it mock nor fail !
Be comforted ! Let Him thy comfort be ;
Balm for all pain, and light for loneliest vale,—
Himself the peace,—the joy,—the company.

TO SEARCH YOU OUT A PLACE.

" The LORD your God . . . Who went in the way before you, to search you out a place."—De. i. 30, 33.

" The LORD went before them by day in a pillar of cloud, to lead them the way ; and by night in a pillar of fire, to give them light ; to go by day and night."—Ex. xiii. 21.

" He maketh me to lie down in green pastures : He leadeth me beside the still waters."—Ps. xxiii. 2.

" He leadeth me in the paths of righteousness for His name's sake."—Ps. xxiii. 3.

HE went, He went before them,
In condescending grace :
Their tents—they needed pitching—
He went to search a place !

He always goes before us !
At least He always would :
To search us out a camp-ground
Which He knows to be good.

To search us out those pastures
Which, unto Him, seem best,
And streams of glad refreshing
Whereby we may be blest.

Thus, though mists gather o'er us,
And much we cannot trace,
We know He goes before us,
To search us out a place.

NOW . . . THROUGH A GLASS.

" What I do thou knowest not now ; but thou shalt know (understand, R.V.) hereafter."—Jno. xiii. 7.

" Thy judgments are a great deep."—Ps. xxxvi. 6.

" O the depth of the riches both of the wisdom and knowledge of God ! how unsearchable are His judgments, and His ways past finding out ! "—Ro. xi. 33.

" Now we see through a glass, darkly ; but then face to face : now I know in part ; but then shall I know even as also I am known."—I Co. xiii. 12.

NOW through a glass, and darkly, do we trace
Things which o'erwhelm, of shadow and of gloom :
How can we know—till Yonder, face to face,
The mystery of full many an opened tomb ?

Now through a glass, and darkly, 'tis we see
The things which come of seeming crushing weight ;
Depths great, unfathomed ; dark with mystery ;
Not to be known till opes the Golden Gate.

Now through a glass ! and darkly ! Yes, ah, yes !
Though this stays not the sob, nor stills the sigh,—
Though it makes not the weight of sorrow less
It brings this balm—we shall know by-and-by.

Now through a glass, and darkly ! Sure 'tis blest
He hath thus writ of holden vision here :
Griefs which o'erwhelm, or graves made in the breast,
All darkly seen till Heaven's light makes clear.

IN JESUS' KEEPING.

" I would not have you to be ignorant, brethren, concerning them which are asleep, that ye sorrow not, even as others which have no hope. For if we believe that Jesus died and rose again, even so them also which sleep in Jesus will God bring with Him."—I Th. iv. 13, 14.

" I know Whom I have believed, and am persuaded that He is able to keep that which I have committed unto Him against that day."—II Ti. i. 12.

" The Lord is thy keeper."—Ps. cxxi. 5.

" He that keepeth thee will not slumber."—Ps. cxxi. 3.

" Now unto Him that is able to keep you from falling, and to present you faultless before the presence of His glory with exceeding joy, to the only wise God our Saviour, be glory and majesty, dominion and power, both now and ever. Amen." —Jude 24, 25.

IN Jesus' keeping we may safely leave them,
Those precious to us, but now veiled away ;
They are at rest, all safe in Jesus sleeping,
Waiting the glad,—the Resurrection Day.

In Jesus' keeping—some we fondly cherish
In distant lands, far over main and sea ;
We would be near—to love and bless and succour ;
Yet, this our comfort—they are kept by Thee !

In Jesus' keeping ! We ourselves commend us
Unto Thy keeping, that we safe may be ;
We have no safety,—no protecting refuge,—
Save as we find security in Thee.

In Jesus' keeping ! this our true ambition,
Thus to be kept upon life's pilgrim road ;
Till safe at last, with risks and dangers ended,
We find ourselves all safe, at home with God.

FAR BETTER.

" To-day shalt thou be with Me in paradise."—Lu. xxiii. 43.

" There the wicked cease from troubling; and there the weary be at rest."—Job iii. 17.

" I am in a strait betwixt two, having a desire to depart, and to be with Christ; which is FAR BETTER."—Phi. i. 23.

" Blessed are the dead which die in the Lord."—Re. xiv. 13.

" We that are in this tabernacle do groan, being burdened: not for that we would be unclothed, but clothed upon, that mortality might be swallowed up of life."—II Co. v. 4.

FAR better to be There—beyond all sorrow,
To be beyond the sin, and stress, and strife;
To be where there can be no dark to-morrow;
Beyond the claims, and cares, of mortal life.

Far better to be There—beyond temptation;
Beyond the scene of conflict, and of strain;
To be in that blest, wondrous habitation
Where ransomed ones can taste no more of pain.

Far better to be There,—with Christ in Glory,—
To know the wondrous bliss of being free,—
Than to have tarried here till years were hoary,
Unless He had designed it so to be.

Far better to be There! Thus we may leave them,
Until there breaks that Resurrection Day,—
When we once more, but with new joy, perceive them,
And share the bliss which shall not pass away

FORGETTING THOSE THINGS.

" Not as though I had already attained, either were already perfect : but I follow after, if that I may apprehend that for which also I am apprehended of Christ Jesus. Brethren, I count not myself to have apprehended : but this one thing I do, forgetting those things which are behind, and reaching forth unto those things which are before, I press toward the mark for the prize of the high calling of God in Christ Jesus." —Phi. iii. 12-14.

" Thanks be unto God, which always causeth us to triumph in Christ."—II Cor. ii. 14.

" And you . . . hath He quickened together with Him, having forgiven you all trespasses."—Col. ii. 13.

FORGETTING those things—those things which are behind,
Those things which eat, and injure, and undo ;
Those things which nag, and chafe upon the mind,—
Forgetting those—and pressing on unto— !

Forgetting those things—those things toward us done,
Those unjust things which truly wounded sore :
Those shadowed things—yes, e'en the darkest one,
Upon them all fast closing memory's door.

Forgetting those things—those things which we regret,—
'Tis not the Spirit bids us on them brood :
Since brooding thus undoing doth beget,
It cannot for the spirit e'er be good.

Forgetting those things—heights gained, and victories won !
Forgetting all, lest progress should be stayed ;
With face well set—the race not fully run,—
We onward press, undaunted, undismayed.

PEACE ON EARTH ?

" Ye shall hear of wars and rumours of wars : see that ye be not troubled : for all these things must come to pass, but the end is not yet."—Matt. xxiv. 6.

" For nation shall rise against nation, and kingdom against kingdom: and there shall be famines, and pestilences, and earthquakes, in divers places."—Matt. xxiv. 7.

" He laid hold on the dragon . . . the Devil, and Satan, and bound him a thousand years . . . that he SHOULD DECEIVE THE NATIONS NO MORE, till the thousand years should be fulfilled."—Re. xx. 2, 3.

NOT " Peace on Earth "—when fear, distrust, suspicion
Loom large and grave on almost every hand ;
Where apprehensiveness is the condition
Obtaining now in almost every land.

Not " Peace on Earth " when statesmen, rulers, pressmen,
Absorb so much of time and talk on war ;
When armaments,—their limits or their building,
Engage, engross, so much, on every shore.

Not " Peace on Earth," when pacts, agreements, treaties,
All,—all are vain, to bring that sense of rest,—
That happy, tranquil, inter-race confiding,—
That mutual trust which would be, oh, so blest.

Not " Peace on Earth ! " For still deceives the nations
The Arch-Deceiver,—not by men discerned :
They see not that 'tis *he* who makes them hostile,—
That such things are of *him* they have not learned.

Not " Peace on Earth "—not yet,—nor ever can be,
Till Christ, the Prince of Peace, shall come again ;
Till Satan, who deceives, is placed in bondage,
No, not till then can " peace on Earth " e'er reign.

FELL ASLEEP.

" They stoned Stephen, calling upon God, and saying, Lord Jesus, receive my spirit. And he kneeled down, and cried with a loud voice, Lord, lay not this sin to their charge. And when he had said this, he FELL ASLEEP."—Ac. vii. 59, 60.

" I would not have you to be ignorant, brethren, concerning them which are asleep."—I Th. iv. 13.

" Them also which sleep in Jesus will God bring with Him."—I Th. iv. 14.

" Some are fallen asleep."—I Co. xv. 6.

HE fell asleep ! He saw in Heaven the Saviour !
" Lord Jesus," cried he, " take my spirit home " ;
His bruised and broken form was now a burden ;
And now he fell asleep, for Christ said " Come " !

They " fell asleep,"—our loved ones from us taken ;
They knew the Saviour,—knew they were forgiven ;
They knew the peace and pardon of " salvation " ;
They knew their everlasting home was Heaven.

They " fell asleep " ! It was not death that took them,—
Nor death that held them in its cold embrace ;
They " fell asleep,"—their spirits went to Jesus ;—
And now they rest in Heaven's dear resting-place.

They " fell asleep "—sweet sleep of the believer !
They " fell asleep,"—and thus, we leave them There :
And we, who wait, look forward to the Morning,—
The Resurrection Morning,—passing fair.

IF I HAD— ?

" Not that I speak in respect of want : for I have learned, in whatsoever state I am, therewith to be content."—Phi. iv. 11.

" I know both how to be abased, and I know how to abound : every where, and in all things I am instructed both to be full and to be hungry, both to abound and to suffer need."—Phi. iv. 12.

" In weariness and painfulness, in watchings often, in hunger and thirst, in fastings often, in cold and nakedness." —II Co. xi. 27.

" Ye have well done, that ye did communicate with my affliction."—Phi. iv. 14.

" Ye know how through infirmity of the flesh I preached the Gospel unto you. . . . If it had been possible, ye would have plucked out your own eyes, and have given them to me."—Ga. iv. 13, 15.

IF I had health of flawless kind,
A perfect frame, which ne'er knew pain,
With health and strength sublime combined,
I wonder——would it all be gain ?

If I had wealth,—delightful, rare,—
An amplitude of things of Earth,—
And knew no need, and felt no care,—
I wonder——what would be its worth ?

If life went by just like a song,
Or like a pleasant dream should be,—
Untroubled through the whole year long,—
Would that be best, my soul, for me ?

I wonder—— ! Yet, my heart knows this—
That pains, and needs, and cares are mine ;
Rough rungs, on which I climb to bliss,
Surpassing ; endless ; sure ; divine.

LO, I AM WITH YOU.

" Lo, I am with you alway, even unto the end of the world (Age)."—Matt. xxviii. 20.

" And remember, I am with you always, DAY BY DAY." —Matt. xxviii. 20 (Weymouth).

" Thou compassest my path and my lying down."—Ps. cxxxix. 3.

" If I take the wings of the morning, and dwell in the uttermost parts of the sea ; EVEN THERE shall Thy hand lead me, and Thy right hand shall hold me."—Ps. cxxxix. 9, 10.

" I will fear no evil : for THOU art with me."—Ps. xxiii. 4.

LO, I am with you ! With you as I promised !
What though ye see Me not, nor feel Me near ?
Lo, I am with you ! rest your heart upon it !
Lo, I am with you ! Always ! Now ! And here !

" Lo, I am with you." Statement more than promise!
Great its salvation—if we take His Word !
Lo, I am with you—Christ the King of glory !
Lo, I am with you,—Jesus, Saviour, Lord.

Lo, I am with you, in the darkest valley !
Lo, I am with you, in life's brightest hour !
Lo, I am with you, in life's deepest sorrow !
With you as well in summer's fairest bower !

Lo, I am with you. Now ! Henceforth ! Forever !
Ye, who are Mine, by precious blood, My own ;
Lo, I am with you,—have this for your comfort :
No hour can be when thou art quite alone.

NO SHADOWS THERE.

" Write, Blessed are the dead which die in the Lord."—Rev. xiv. 13.

" To-day shalt thou be with Me in paradise."—Luke xxiii. 43.

" With Christ : which is far better."—Phil. i. 23.

" There shall be no more curse . . . they shall see His face . . . and there shall be no night there."—Rev. xxii. 3-5.

NO shadows There ! They joyfully behold Him !
No cloud to dim their vision of His face !
No jarring note to mar the holy rapture,
The perfect bliss of that most blessèd place.

No burdens There ! These all are gone forever !
No weary nights, no long or dragging days !
No sighings There, or secret, silent longings,—
For all is now unutterable praise.

No conflicts There ! No evil hosts assailing !
Such warfare past—forever made to cease ;
No tempter's voice is heard within those portals ;
No foe lurks there to break the perfect peace.

No sorrows There ! no sadness and no weeping !
Tears wiped away—all radiant now each face ;
Music and song, in happy holy blending,
Fill all the courts of that sweet resting-place.

WITH CHRIST.

" I am in a strait betwixt two, having a desire to depart, and to be with Christ ; which is far better."—Phil. i. 23.

" To-day shalt thou be with ME in paradise."—Luke xxiii. 43.

" Them also which sleep in Jesus will God bring with Him."—II Thess. iv. 14.

WITH Christ ! brief word ; all human thought transcending :
To tell its bliss the mortal tongue must fail :
Earth hath no speech, and mind no comprehending,
For that blest state which reigns within the veil.

With Christ ! set free from human limitation ;
Free from its pangs, its burdens, and its woe ;
Free, ever free, oh, glad emancipation !
No sense of frailty henceforth now to know.

With Christ ! immune from sadness, sin, and sorrow ;
To share no more Earth's anguish, pain, and tears ;
Nor yet to have one thought about a morrow,
Since morrows come not where there are no years.

With Christ ! What bliss ! Glad, unalloyed communion !
What hallowed joys with loved ones gathered there !
With choice celestial spirits ! oh, what union !
With Christ ! Blest place ! Blest home beyond compare !

WITH THE LORD.

" We are confident, I say, and willing rather to be absent from the body, and to be present with the Lord."—II Cor. v. 8.

" I am in a strait betwixt two, having a desire to depart, and to be with Christ : which is far better."—Phi. i. 23.

" That where I am, there ye may be also."—Jno. xiv. 3.

" WITH the Lord " ! Not " gone," nor " passed away " ;
Absent from us 'tis true, and we them miss ;
But they have now begun their Endless Day,—
Safe with the Lord,—in realms of ceaseless bliss.

" With the Lord " ! Not 'neath the sod they rest :
Nobly, till strength was spent, they ran life's race :
Now with the Lord, and thus sublimely blest,
Wait they with Him, in Heaven's great homing-place.

" With the Lord " ! Sweet comfort it doth bring !
Sufferings past,—with them we know 'tis well ;
HE is their all in all,—their everything ;
Heaven—the hallowed home wherein they dwell.

" With the Lord " ! We would not wish them here,—
Tearful or sad though we at times may be ;
They are with Him,—in Heaven's unsullied sphere,—
Joying in holy, sweet felicity.

THE BLESSÈD DEAD.

" And I heard a voice from heaven saying unto me, Write, Blessed are the dead which die in the Lord from henceforth : Yea, saith the Spirit, that they may rest from their labours ; and their works do follow them."—Rev. xiv. 13.

" Having a desire to depart and to be with Christ ; which is far better."—Phil. i. 23.

" I would not have you to be ignorant, brethren, concerning them which are asleep, that ye sorrow not . . . for if we believe that Jesus died and rose again, even so them also which sleep in Jesus will God bring with Him. . . . We which are alive and remain shall be caught up together with them . . . so shall we ever be with the Lord."—I Th. iv. 13-17.

" THE Blessèd dead ! " for so He sweetly calls them ;
The blessèd dead, who in the Lord have died,
While from us to the Heavenly Home now taken,
'Twixt whom and us death's stream doth now divide,—

They are at rest ! their labours now are ended,—
The earthly toil and task for them are done ;
Their course is finished,—warfare fully over ;
Their race, their noble race, completely run.

And now their works, their God-owned works do follow ;
Their works still live, though they have onward passed :
They lived for Him, for Him they truly laboured,
And He ordains that now their works shall last.

Dear, blessèd dead ! 'Tis not as dead we view them !
They live beyond,—in Heaven's abiding place ;
And we shall meet, when our course, too, is finished,
And share the fadeless joys of matchless grace.

WITHOUT CLOUDS.

" A morning without clouds."—II Sa. xxiii. 4.

" There shall be no night there ; and they need no candle, neither light of the sun ; for the Lord God giveth them light."—Rev. xxii. 5.

NO clouds are There ! No mystery and no shadow ;
No dark enigmas—hard to understand !
No tears are There, no weeping and no sadness,—
For There—it is a cloudless, tearless land.

No clouds ! No darksome clouds of lonely sorrow ;
No tragic hours of eating, mental pain ;
No consciousness of human desolation,—
Nor agony of heart can come again.

No clouds of anxious thought about some morrow,—
One's own, or others, e'er again can be ;
No slow, incessant, taxing, wearing burden,—
Since from the mortal frame all There are free.

No clouds ! No clouds at all ! The Saviour's presence,—
Seraphic music, and angelic song,—
And bliss, beyond all human comprehending,
Are 'mongst the joys which to those There belong.

WE'LL MEET AGAIN

"The dead in Christ shall rise first: Then we which are alive and remain shall be caught up together with them in the clouds, to meet the Lord in the air: and so shall we ever be with the Lord."—1 Thess. iv. 16, 17.

"Cast not away therefore your confidence, which hath great recompence of reward. For ye have need of patience . . . For yet a little while, and He that shall come will come, and will not tarry."—Heb. x. 35-37.

WE'LL meet again – the loved ones gone before us –
  In that bright realm – the land of light and love;
It may be that e'en now they're watching o'er us,
  And longing for the time we'll meet above.

We'll meet again – of that we may be certain,
  In that bright Home so wondrous and so fair,
Whose glories, veiled to us as by a curtain,
  Through God's redeeming grace we are to share.

We'll meet where neither sadnesses nor sorrows
  Shall for one moment rob the heart of joy;
Where there shall be no dark uncertain morrows,
  Or aught whatever to the bliss destroy.

Ah, yes, we'll meet again in that bright glory;
  How wondrous it will be to talk things o'er,
And to begin a fresh, but never-ending story
  Of life which shall endure for evermore.

WITH HIM IN TROUBLE

"I will be with him in trouble."—Ps. xci. 15.

"When they in their trouble did turn unto the Lord . . . He was found of them."—2 Chron. xv. 4.

"The Lord will be a refuge for the oppressed, a refuge in times of trouble."—Ps. ix. 9.

WONDERFUL promise – dear child of the
Kingdom –
"I will be with him in trouble, I will;
With him in hours of the direst affliction;
With him in times of unspeakable ill."

"I will be with him! I will not forsake him!"
Wonderful Presence – unseen, but so nigh:
Wonderful fact – that He companies with us –
Faithful, unchanging, and standing nearby.

With us – to keep us from heart-break and sorrow;
With us – to teach us some things we should know;
With us – to give us what we cannot borrow –
Treasures from darkness, and triumph in woe.

Trouble there must be! 'Tis linked with this promise!
Trouble *must* be – not to blight but to bless;
Trouble to show us the wondrous salvation
Of His dear Presence in all our distress.

GOD EVER CARES.

"When my spirit was overwhelmed within me, then Thou knewest my path."—Psalm cxlii. 3.

"I looked on my right hand, and beheld, but there was no man that would know me: refuge failed me; no man cared for my soul."—Psalm cxlii. 4.

"The eternal God is thy refuge."—Deut. xxxiii. 27.

"Casting all your care upon Him; for *He careth for you.*"**—I Peter v. 7.**

GOD EVER CARES! Not only in life's summer,
When skies are bright and days are long and glad:
He cares as much when life is draped in winter,
And heart doth feel bereft, and lone, and sad.

GOD EVER CARES! His heart is ever tender;
His love doth never fail nor show decay:
The loves of earth, though strong and deep, may perish,—
But His shall never, never pass away.

GOD EVER CARES! And thus when life is lonely,
When blessings one time prized are growing dim,—
The heart may find a sweet and sunny shelter,—
A refuge and a resting-place in Him.

GOD EVER CARES! And Time can never change Him;—
His nature is to care, and love, and bless;
And drearest, darkest, emptiest days afford Him
But means to make more sweet His own caress.

THE CUP HE GIVETH.

" O My Father, if this cup may not pass away from Me, except I drink it, Thy will be done."—Matt. xxvi. 42.

" The cup which My Father hath given Me."—John xviii. 11.

THE cup which my Father hath given me !
Shall I count it bitter ? ah, nay ;
Though full, oh, so full of sorrow,
And deepest heart-agony.
I cannot tell why He hath given it,—
And may not know till that Day,
When the tears and the griefs and the anguish
For ever have passed away.

The cup which my Father hath given me
Was mingled by Love Divine ;
He did not give it to mock me,
Instead of the choicest wine :
And perchance, perchance in the Glory,
When all things are understood,
I shall say, as I cannot meanwhile,
" This cup was meant unto good."

And so, I do trust my Father,—
And smile, through my tears, to Him
He knows, ah, He knows how costly
This cup—sorrow-filled to the brim.
And e'en as I seek to drink it,
Through His all-sufficient grace,
Perhaps I shall see more clearly
The light of His blessèd face.

Enough—that His hand hath given it !
The hand that gave all for me
Can never hold aught but blessing,
And blessing in rich degree.
Dear hand ! dear hand of my Father !
Dear hand that my Saviour gave !
I tenderly now would clasp it,
And ask to be strong and brave.

SORROW UPON SORROW.

" Yet I supposed it necessary to send to you Epaphroditus, my brother, and companion in labour, and fellow-soldier . . . he longed after you all, and was full of heaviness, because that ye had heard that he had been sick. For, indeed, he was sick nigh unto death : but God had mercy on him ; and not on him only, but on me also, lest I should have sorrow upon sorrow."—Phil. ii. 25-27.

" I have great heaviness and continual sorrow in my heart."—Rom. ix. 2.

DEATH threatened ! It meant going Home ;
And Heaven was better far than Rome :
" But, oh, the anguish and the woe.
Epaphroditus, if you go ;
How deep my overwhelming grief ;
Where, then, shall I e'er find relief ? "

Death threatens still ! Then it doth come,
And we are stupified, and numb :
Our best belovèd snatched away,
And desolate hangs the brightest day :
And sorrow upon sorrow weighs,
And, broken quite, we cannot praise.

And is it right such grief to bear,—
Such sorrow we with none can share ;
Such anguish—we can only cry,—
And, stricken, unto Him say, " Why ? " :
Yet find no answering note is given,—
No explanation come from Heaven.

Well, human, God-made,—if intense
We live and love, the recompense,
When death's cold hand some loved one takes,
Is this—the human heart oft breaks,—
And knows full well life ne'er can be
The same as in its yesterday.

Yet God is good ! Upbraid ? Ah, no !
He reads the anguish and the woe ;
The broken heart He gently tends ;
The life bereft He soothes, befriends :
And Time and Grace—great healing arts,
He uses for our broken hearts.

SORROW'S SANCTIFIER.

" Surely He hath borne our griefs, and carried our sorrows."—Isa. liii. 4.

" Blessed are they that mourn : for they shall be comforted."—Mat. v. 4.

" In all their affliction He was afflicted, and the angel of His presence saved them."—Isa. lxiii. 9.

" Seek Him that . . . turneth the shadow of death into the morning . . . the Lord is His name."—Amos v. 8.

O SOUL bereft,—thou mournest much
The absent face,—the old-time touch,—
The now stilled voice,—the presence gone ;
And life seems so bereft and lone.

But Christ is near ! unchanged by years !
He doth not chide thee for thy tears !
Thy heavy grief—thy anguished cry,
He can subdue and sanctify.

He comes not now to take away
Remembrances of yesterday ;
Not to obliterate mem'ries blest
Of one now safe with Him at rest.

Thy bleeding heart-wound He can heal,
Though vacancy thou long dost feel ;
And sorrowing sense may help Him be
A dearer Presence unto thee.

Speak much with Him,—for, while He knows,
The telling Him doth bring repose ;
By contact oft,—communion blest,
The heart will find a deeper rest.

IT MATTERS TO GOD.

" Casting all your care upon Him ; for it matters to God about you."—I Peter v. 7.

" He that toucheth you toucheth the apple of His eye."—Zec. ii. 8.

" The Father Himself loveth you, because ye have loved Me."—Jno. xvi. 27.

" Your heavenly Father knoweth."—Mat. vi. 32.

IT matters to God ! precious comfort in sorrow ;
It matters to God—soothing solace in tears ;
It matters to God—all about the to-morrow,
The uncertain track, and the long-stretching years.

It matters to God all about the sore heart-ache,—
He knoweth the cause, as He holdeth the cure ;
And if He sees best not to heal quick the heart-break,
'Tis sure He'll give exquisite grace to endure.

It matters to God—all about what perplexes,—
The problems and tangles we cannot undo ;
The burdens which press and the thing which sore vexes,—
They matter to Him,—and He'll see us right through.

It matters to God ! This brings comfort and healing,—
Thus heart will not under its burden give way,—
For into its inmost recesses comes stealing,
" It matters to God—yea, it matters to-day " !

AS A MOTHER COMFORTETH.

" As one whom his mother comforteth, so will I comfort you."—Isa. lxvi. 13.

" To comfort all that mourn . . . to give unto them beauty for ashes, the oil of joy for mourning, the garment of praise for the spirit of heaviness."—Isa. lxi. 2, 3.

" The God of all comfort, Who comforteth us in all our tribulation."—II Co. i. 3, 4.

WHEN tears are falling, and mind is sad ;
When life seems robbed of the bliss it had ;
When heart feels empty, bereft, and lone ;
When treasured joys are no longer known ;
It is then, it is then, He will draw *so* near
To comfort, and strengthen, and soothe, and cheer !

He knows the anguish, the grief, the pain !
He understandeth the tears that rain !
The heart's deep hunger—its loneliness :
The love so craving the fond caress !
It is then, it is then, that He will draw near
To lovingly, tenderly dry each tear.

. . . . . .

Will He come as King—with a great array—
With sovereign splendour and grand display ?
He comes not thus when He comes to bless
His dear one in broken-heartedness !
Ah no—as a mother—the best, most dear—
To soothe and to comfort will He draw near !

A MAN OF SORROWS.

" He is despised and rejected of men ; a man of sorrows, and acquainted with grief. . . . Surely He hath borne our griefs, and carried our sorrows."—Isa. liii. 3, 4.

" I have surely seen the affliction of My people . . . for I know their sorrows ; and I am come down to deliver them."—Ex. iii. 7, 8.

" When Jesus therefore saw her weeping . . . He groaned in the spirit, and was troubled . . . Jesus wept." —Jno. xi. 33-35.

" We have not an high priest which cannot be touched with the feeling of our infirmities. . . . "—He. iv. 15.

FROM heaven He looked ; He heard the prisoner groaning :
Angelic choirs dulled not their plaintive cry ;
He was so touched,—touched with their tragic moaning—
He could not stay ! He had to come ! To die !

On earth He shared, minutely, human sorrow ;
He groaned ; was troubled ; wept—e'en at the grave
No strength o'er grief did He, unhuman, borrow,
Nor stoic power to make Him strangely brave.

And His own life—though He was Prince of Glory,—
Was filled with grief—grief words can never pen :
" A Man of Sorrows "—who could write the story
Of sorrows deeper far than come to men ?

To-day He knows, He reads, He shares my anguish ;
Those things I deeply feel but cannot tell :
Nor does He leave me in my grief to languish,—
Nor in my human woe to mutely dwell.

He loves ! He cares ! Minutely comprehendeth !
And from His heart to mine there floweth balm :
And if 'tis not yet time that sorrow endeth,
My heart, 'midst all its grief, may know His calm.

THOU REMAINEST.

" LORD, Thou hast been our dwelling-place in all generations."—Psalm xc. 1.

" Jesus Christ—the same yesterday, and to-day, and for ever."—Heb. xiii. 8.

" They shall perish, but THOU REMAINEST ; **and they all shall wax old as doth a garment ; and as a vesture shalt Thou fold them up, and they shall be changed : but Thou art the same, and Thy years shall not fail."—Heb. i. 11, 12.**

WHEN from my life the old-time joys have vanished—
Treasures, once mine, I may no longer claim,—
This truth may feed my hungry heart and famished :—
Lord, THOU REMAINEST ! THOU art still the same !

When streams have dried, those streams of glad refreshing,—
Friendships so blest, so pure, so rich, so free ;
When sun-kissed skies give place to clouds depressing,—
Lord, THOU REMAINEST ! Still my heart hath THEE.

When strength hath failed, and feet, now worn and weary,
On gladsome errands may no longer go,—
Why should I sigh, or let the days be dreary ?
Lord, THOU REMAINEST ! Couldst Thou more bestow ?

Thus through life's days,—whoe'er or what may fail me,—
Friends, friendships, joys,—in small or great degree,—
Songs may be mine,—no sadness need assail me,
Since THOU REMAINEST, and my heart hath THEE.

GOD MY EXCEEDING JOY.

" Lord, to whom shall we go ? Thou hast the words of eternal life."—John vi. 68.

" Whom have I in heaven but Thee ? and there is none upon earth that I desire beside Thee."—Psalm lxxiii. 25.

" The Kingdom of God is not meat and drink ; but righteousness, and peace, and joy in the Holy Ghost."—Rom. xiv. 17.

" Then will I go unto the altar of God, unto GOD MY EXCEEDING JOY.**"—Psalm xliii. 4.**

THERE is a joy—all other joys exceeding,—
A quiet joy, which Time can ne'er destroy :
A joy through tears,—through pain,—through sore heart-bleeding ;
This joy is God—" God my exceeding Joy ! "

When bitter words have reached me with their stinging,—
Words base, unworthy, undeserved and wrong,—
" God—my exceeding joy"—within up-springing—
My heart, through Him, hath still its music song.

When crushing blows upon me thick are falling,
And, sore and broken, sink I on life's way,—
I shall arise from 'neath such weight appalling,—
" God my exceeding joy " shall be my stay.

When shadows fall, and death hath loved ones taken,
And, for a time, songs may not voice employ,
This deathless song its echoes sweet shall waken
Still deep within—" God my exceeding joy."

SOMEWHERE.

" In My Father's house are many mansions."—Jno. xiv. 2.

" We which are alive and remain, shall be caught up together with them in the clouds."—I Th. iv. 17.

" And they sung a new song, saying, Thou art worthy to take the book, and to open the seals thereof : for Thou wast slain, and hast redeemed us to God by Thy blood, out of every kindred, and tongue, and people, and nation ; and hast made us unto our God kings and priests : and we shall reign on the earth."—Rev. v. 9, 10.

SOMEWHERE amidst the sea of radiant faces
In yon celestial Home ;
Somewhere amidst its vast unbounded spaces,
Where, perhaps, we may roam :
Somewhere I'll meet the one I fondly cherish,
And whom I anguished miss—
There to renew a bond that ne'er shall perish
In Heaven's eternal bliss.

Somewhere within that place of holy rapture,
Where is no night nor need,—
Not through some quest of mine shall I recapture
That for which now I bleed :
But in that Home of such surpassing splendour,—
Heaven's unsullied place,—
I may renew those holy ties and tender,
Through the dear Father's grace.

Somewhere,—yes, somewhere,—when what now is holden
Shall be forever clear ;
When we shall enter on that life so golden,—
Heav'n's holy, happy sphere :
Somewhere, yes, somewhere—'midst those realms abiding,
We may have touch most rare ;
Taste hallowed joys of God's ungrudged providing,—
And bliss undreamt-of share.

THE HEART KNOWETH ITS OWN——?

" The heart knoweth his own bitterness : and a stranger doth not intermeddle with his joy."—Prov. xiv. 10.

" What man knoweth the things of a man, save the spirit of man which is in him ? "--I Cor. ii. 11.

" Job answered and said, Even to-day is my complaint bitter : my stroke is heavier than my groaning. . . . But He knoweth the way that I take (the way that is with me—*marg.*) : when He hath tried me, I shall come forth as gold."—Job xxiii. 1, 2, 10.

NOT bitterness ! ah, no, that word is not quite worthy :
And yet,—and yet,—there hath no other known
The overwhelming sense of lonely sadness
Now thine, my soul ;—thou sharest it alone.

Think it not strange that human loves must fail thee !
That human minds—the finest—cannot know :
That human hearts are futile to avail thee
The sense of balm from reading full thy woe.

Think it not strange ! Thy God Who made thee gave thee
Vast inward depths—yet which none may explore
Save thee, thyself,—yea, depths for joy or sorrow,—
And, to these inner realms, none pass the door :

None—save the Lord ! the Comforter ! the Spirit !
He, with thyself, the deepest depths can share !
And, soul of mine, thou shalt not e'er go under,
If thou wouldst oft-times have Him join thee there.

GATHER ME UP.

" When my father and my mother forsake me, then the LORD will take (Heb. ' gather ') me up."—Ps. xxvii. 10.

" He shall feed His flock like a shepherd : He shall gather the lambs with His arm, and carry them in His bosom, and shall gently lead those that are with young."—Is. xl. 11.

" O Jerusalem, Jerusalem . . . how often would I have gathered thy children together, even as a hen gathereth her chickens. . . ."—Mat. xxiii. 37.

GATHER me up—as a chalice all shattered ;
Piece me together—once more make me whole :
Gather the fragments which now are so scattered ;
Give me completeness again in my soul.

Gather me up—as a lamb, lost and lonely—
Bleating for comfort, and compassed with need :
Great Shepherd-heart—to have sense of Thee only—
That is the solace for which I would plead.

Gather me up—as an orphan forsaken,
Shorn of its parents, and broken in grief :
Just to be gathered, and by Those Arms taken—
Exquisite soothing,—amazing relief !

Thus in my brokenness, anguish and sorrow,
Will not He " gather " me ? Doth not He care ?
Will not He bear me through life's long to-morrow,
And joys unending at last with me share ?

ON JESUS' BOSOM.

" A Man of sorrows, and acquainted with grief. . . . " —Isa. liii. 3.

" Touched with the feeling of our infirmities."—Heb. iv. 15.

" Now there was leaning ON JESUS' BOSOM one of His disciples, whom Jesus loved."—John xiii. 23.

ON JESUS' BOSOM—nowhere else is found
Balm for all wounds, and solace for all tears;
Calm 'mid the clouds which gather thickly round,
Peace from the pain which lingers through life's years.

ON JESUS' BOSOM! Broken, weary, yet
Finding His welcome—loving, tender, sure:
Soothed by His kiss; some sorrows helped forget;
Strengthened for those which heart must still endure.

ON JESUS' BOSOM! Truly welcomed there!
Warmed by His love,—His tender, sweet embrace:
Made strong, once more, life's overweight to bear;
Lightened again by radiance from His face.

ON JESUS' BOSOM! This my refuge be
Till shadowed days for evermore are past;
Till, in the home Christ now prepares for me,
I find my everlasting place at last.

UNDERNEATH and EVERLASTING.

" The eternal God is thy refuge, and UNDERNEATH ARE THE EVERLASTING ARMS."—**Deut. xxxiii. 27.**

CHILD of God, forlorn and weary,
Doth the way seem overlong ?
Are the skies above thee dreary,
And thou hast no heart for song ?
Pause awhile ! and think, and ponder,—
There are Arms outstretched for thee !
Arms that tell of love far fonder
Than earth's fondest love could be !

Arms of Jesus,—Everlasting ;
Arms that never weary grow ;
We, our loads upon them casting,
Cannot tire them. Cannot. No !
Open arms,—outstretched, inviting
To the weary, much-worn saint,
With the strain of constant fighting
In the heavenly warfare, faint.

Arms outstretched ! And oh ! the wonder,
Underneath thee, they are there !
Always, *always*, ALWAYS under,
Thee to catch and thee to bear.
'Neath thee in thy sorest trial,
'Neath thee in thy deepest woe,
'Neath thee should thy life's sun-dial
Tell that setting sun is low.

Outstretched ! Tireless ! And unfailing !
Underneath—these Arms are spread !
Strong ! Their strength so all-availing !
Softer yet than infant's bed !
Such the Arms that now would hold thee :
Have thee know their perfect rest ;
Have thee find, as they enfold thee,
Quenchless love on Jesu's breast.

UNFAILING YET

"Be strong and of a good courage, fear not, nor be afraid of them: for the Lord thy God, He it is that doth go with thee; He will not fail thee, nor forsake thee."—Deut. xxxi. 6.

"There hath not failed one word of all His good promise."—1 Kings viii. 56.

"Forsake me not when my strength faileth."—Ps. lxxi. 9.

UNFAILING yet – though all my hopes are shattered,
  Though fondest dreams or plans now cannot be,
Though links of life are gone, or now are scattered,
  Unfailing yet – His love and care for me.

Unfailing yet – though life has strangely altered,
  Though substance is not as in days gone by,
Though friends have failed, or in their love have faltered,
  Unfailing yet – His love can satisfy.

Unfailing yet – though mortal flesh be failing,
  Though steps grow slow, or sight be growing dim,
Though house of clay in many ways be ailing,
  Unfailing yet – the consciousness of Him.

Unfailing yet – though much we once did cherish
  Must needful pass or fall into decay –
His love unfailing will not change or perish,
  And there awaits the Everlasting Day.

THE LAND OF NO NEED.

" And I saw no temple therein : for the Lord God Almighty and the Lamb are the temple of it. And the city had no need of the sun, neither of the moon, to shine in it : for the glory of God did lighten it, and the Lamb is the light thereof."—Rev. xxi. 22-23.

" In the midst of the street of it, and on either side of the river, was there the tree of life, which bare twelve manner of fruits, and yielded her fruit every month. . . . There shall be no more curse. . . . They shall see His face. . . . And there shall be no night there : and they need no candle, neither light of the sun : for the Lord God giveth them light : and they shall reign for ever and ever."—Rev. xxii. 2-5.

NO need of the sun in that glory-filled land,—
The sun would itself there be dim !
That land where the shadows or twilight ne'er come,—
Where the light and the glory are " Him."

No need for the moon in that wonderful land,—
For there—it can never be night ;
No need of the candle for those who are there,—
The Lord Himself giveth them light.

Unspeakable land,—where all needs such as these,—
And all other needs cannot be ;
How wonderful, There, in such glory to dwell,—
Such exquisite beauty to see.

The Land of no need ! Oh, how good to be there !
To tried, weary pilgrims how blest !
No need e'en for faith in that rapture-filled land,—
No need—but to worship and rest.

THEN—FACE TO FACE.

" Now we see through a glass, darkly ; but then face to face : now I know in part ; but then shall I know even as also I am known."—I Cor. xiii. 12.

" Blessed are the dead which die in the Lord."—Rev. xiv. 13.

" They shall see His face. . . . "—Rev. xxii. 4.

THEN—face to face ! No hindered, holden vision ;
No twilight reading in that full-orbed day ;
No erring judgment ; no wrong, rash decision ;
Then shall uncertainty have fully passed away.

Then—face to face ! No mystery then o'er sorrow,—
Things so appalling that we oft are numb :
No mystery then ! oh, clear and gladsome morrow,—
What rest, what bliss, when thou at last shall come !

Then—face to face ! Clear then the tragic trials,—
Now oft the lot of those intense for Him :
Saints who here drink the full of bitter vials,—
Then, then shall know what here, at best, is dim.

Then—face to face ! Here—oft the baffling story ;
To finite minds all cannot here be shewn ;
But—when doth burst the Everlasting Glory
Then we shall know as we e'en now are known.

THEN SHALL I KNOW.

" *Then shall I know,* **even as also I am known."— I Cor. xiii. 12.**

" What I do thou knowest not now ; but thou shalt know hereafter."—John xiii. 7.

" Then face to face."—I Cor. xiii. 12.

" THEN shall I know ! " and things now dark,
mysterious,—
Will all unfolded be :
And I shall understand things—seen as evil—
Wrought out God's best for me.

" Then shall I know " the meaning of life's
sorrow,—
Its grief ; its tears ; its pain :
And I shall then perceive,—no more through
shadow,—
Life's loss transformed to gain !

" Then shall I know " how God, the great Refiner,
Through fierce affliction's heat
Was cleansing, purifying, and ennobling,
For Heaven to make me meet.

" Then shall I know "—not now as in earth's
twilight,—
But darkly,—and—oft guessed ;
I shall behold ! and understand ! and **worship** !
And own that all was best.

THERE.

" In My Father's house are many mansions."—Jno. xiv. 2.

" To depart, and to be with Christ ; which is far better." —Phil. i. 23.

" I would not have you to be ignorant, brethren, concerning them which are asleep, that ye sorrow not, even as others which have no hope. For if we believe that Jesus died and rose again, even so them also which sleep in Jesus will God bring with Him."—I Th. iv. 13, 14.

NOT 'neath the sod, in yon green acre, lies
The one ye so much miss ;
The Father's House, beyond the bright, blue skies,
Is now the place of bliss.

There—shadows come not ; grief and tears are past ;
And every sense of pain :
And joys are there, which ever more shall last,
For—night comes ne'er again.

Weep not,—belovèd,—save to get relief;
With those There all is well !
And smiles of peace will radiate through thy grief
As thou on Heaven dost dwell.

A little while,—perchance but weeks, or days,—
Till HE again shall come ;
Yea, any hour He may the glad shout raise,—
One moment,—and then—HOME !

Reunion then ! but richer than below !
A fuller life then ours !
A perfect " touch,"—beyond all we did know
In earth's sublimest hours.

MY TEARS.

" Put Thou my tears into Thy bottle : are they not in Thy book ? "—Ps. lvi. 8.

" I have heard thy prayer, I have seen thy tears."—Isa. xxxviii. 5.

" And God shall wipe away all tears from their eyes."—Rev. vii. 17.

I READ in God's dear Book He has a bottle,—
Wherein, as pass the slowly-rolling years,
He places, one by one, the crystal pearls,—
Those drops which He Himself doth call my " tears."

I thank Him for this means to ease my sorrow,—
The flood, the fount,—which oft doth soothe my grief :
The soft, unbitter rain, which falls so gently,—
And, falling, brings my bosom such relief.

I thank Him that His heart devised this fountain ;
And that its healing balm He understands :
That, too, the sacred thing He calls His " bottle "
Is not with angels, but is in *His* hands.

And so, when bursts the flood-gates of my bosom,
When, overwhelmed, it will not be restrained,—
God's bottle is my comfort, and my solace,—
My tears are there : those tears my heart hath rained.

HIS COMPASSIONS FAIL NOT.

" It is of the LORD'S mercies that we are not consumed, because His compassions fail not. They are new every morning."—Lam. iii. 22.

" Like as a father pitieth his children, so the LORD pitieth them that fear Him."—Psalm ciii. 13.

" For we have not an high priest which cannot be touched with the feeling of our infirmities."—Heb. iv. 15.

HIS compassions fail not ! change not with the years !
He doth read the meaning of life's hidden tears :
Knows, with tenderest feeling, anguish hid away—
Griefs not oft unfolded ; things words fail to say.

His compassions fail not ! others oft-times do :
Hearts responsive, loyal,—are, at most, but few ;
Hopes and aspirations hearts so much engage
That they scarce are fitted griefs to help assuage.

His compassions fail not ! Never ! Never ! Nay !
Trusted ones may fail us—dearest pass away !
But throughout life's journey, howe'er long it be,
Will God's sweet compassions flow unceasingly.

Breaking heart ! draw near Him ! tell to Him thy grief !
He can give thee comfort—soothing, balm, relief ;
Thy lone, dark, deep sorrow He would fully share,
Lead thee to His bosom—give thee solace there.

IT MATTERS TO HIM

"Casting all your care upon Him; for it matters to Him about you."—1 Pet. v. 7.

"No man cared for my soul. I cried unto thee, O Lord: I said, Thou art my refuge and my portion in the land of the living."—Ps. cxlii. 4, 5.

"The Lord redeemeth the soul of His servants: and none of them that trust in Him shall be desolate."—Ps. xxxiv. 22.

IT matters to Him! Oh, wonderful solace!
  It matters to Him – my God on the throne!
It matters to Him – unspeakable comfort,
  Whatever my need – it is all to Him known.

'Tis He Who hath made me: 'tis He understands me:
  And all that is complex within me He reads:
My heart with its manifold hunger He knoweth;
  It matters to Him that it suffers such needs.

It matters to Him! Thus I ne'er am quite lonely;
  The deep things I feel all come under His care:
The pains and the pangs, and the tears and the sorrows –
  They matter to Him – and He doth them all share.

It matters to Him! Thus with much so uncertain –
  The present perplexing – the future so dim –
My heart is made strong, and my spirit is tranquil,
  And this is my comfort – "It matters to Him".

HE SATISFIETH.

" Oh that one would give me drink of the water of the well of Beth-lehem."—II Sam. xxiii. 15.

" O satisfy us early with . . . "—Psalm xc. 14.

" HE SATISFIETH the longing soul."—Psalm cvii. 9.

HE SATISFIETH ! Satisfieth longings !
Those longings which, ourselves, we cannot still,
He satisfieth ! Yea, God satisfieth !
So great, so grand, so wonderful His skill.

HE SATISFIETH when the heart is lonely ;
When treasured loves are lost, or far away ;
How infinite His love, and oh, how tender,—
How sweet the solace He can then convey.

HE SATISFIETH when life's sky is clouded ;
When cherished hopes have found an early grave ;
When streams have dried, and joys, long ours, have perished ;
HE SATISFIETH ! thus we may be brave.

HE SATISFIETH ! Yea, He doth not mock us !
The longing soul He meeteth not in vain ;
The bleeding heart, the life bereft and broken,
He, He alone, can heal of inward pain.

THE FATHER'S HOUSE.

"I will dwell in the house of the LORD for ever."—Psalm xxiii. 6.

"In My Father's house **are many mansions."—John xiv. 2.**

"There shall in no wise enter into it anything that defileth."—Rev. xxi. 27.

THE FATHER'S HOUSE ! Oh say,—what will it be ?
Love ! Perfect love ! And bliss—eternally !
No lonely hearts ! no hunger, deep and sore !
Grief, pain, and sadness—then for ever o'er.

THE FATHER'S HOUSE !—But not a house alone ;
A HOME,—where hearts shall evermore be one :
Where love's sweet language shall the music be ;
No sin to mar the heavenly harmony.

THE FATHER'S HOUSE ! No desolation there !
For hearts with hearts the fullest love will share
And fellowship, from limits then set free,
A holy, everlasting joy will be.

THE FATHER'S HOUSE ! Oh home so wondrous fair !
What will it be—to be forever there ?
Sweet prospect now,—that, through Redeeming Grace,
Home waits to welcome with its long embrace.